The Everything Book of HORSES & PONIES

Author **Andrea Mills**
Consultant **Dr. Ruth Wonfor**
Educational consultant **Jenny Lane-Smith**

DK LONDON
Senior editor **Satu Hämeenaho-Fox**
Senior designer **Elaine Hewson**
US Senior editor **Shannon Beatty**
Pre-production producer **Dragana Puvacic**
Senior producer **Amy Knight**
Jacket designer **Eleanor Bates**
Jacket co-ordinator **Francesca Young**
Managing editor **Penny Smith**
Managing art editor **Mabel Chan**
Creative director **Helen Senior**
Publishing director **Sarah Larter**

DK DELHI
Assistant editors **Shalini Agrawal,
Shambhavi Thatte**
Art editors **Kartik Gera, Seepiya Sahni**
Senior designer **Nidhi Mehra**
Picture researcher **Sumedha Chopra**
DTP designer **Syed Md Farhan**
Managing editor **Alka Thakur Hazarika**
Managing art editor **Romi Chakraborty**
Delhi team head **Malavika Talukder**

First American edition, 2019
Published in the United States by DK Publishing
345 Hudson Street, New York, New York 10014

Published in Great Britain by Dorling Kindersley
Limited. A catalog record for this book is available
from the Library of Congress.
ISBN: 978-1-4654-8011-8

Printed in China

A WORLD OF IDEAS:
SEE ALL THERE IS TO KNOW

www.dk.com

Contents

Welcome to the wonderful world of horses and ponies!

World of horses

Horses are loved throughout the world, but do you know which tamed horses and which feral (living wild) varieties come from each continent?

Domestic horses

Domestic, or tamed, horses have been around in Asia for about 6,000 years. They are now found on every continent except Antarctica.

North America

Quarter horse

Horses were brought to the Americas by European settlers.

South America

Wild horses

There are very few true wild horses living in the world. Feral horses are usually descended from domestic horses.

Falabella

Falabellas are from Argentina. They are one of the smallest horses in the world.

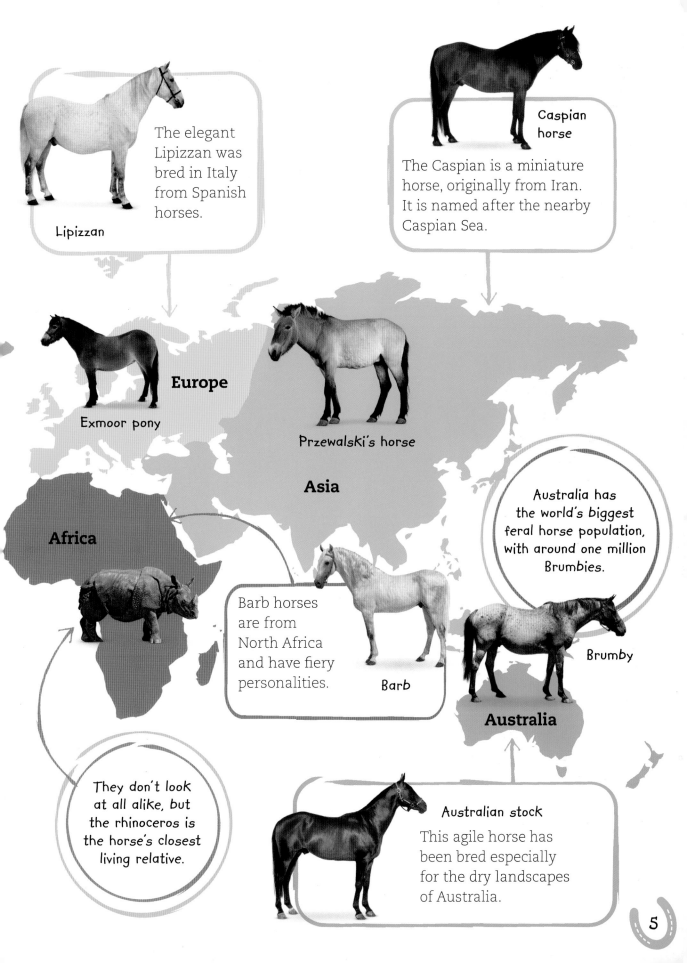

The elegant Lipizzan was bred in Italy from Spanish horses.

Lipizzan

Caspian horse

The Caspian is a miniature horse, originally from Iran. It is named after the nearby Caspian Sea.

Europe

Exmoor pony

Przewalski's horse

Asia

Africa

Australia has the world's biggest feral horse population, with around one million Brumbies.

Barb horses are from North Africa and have fiery personalities.

Barb

Brumby

Australia

They don't look at all alike, but the rhinoceros is the horse's closest living relative.

Australian stock

This agile horse has been bred especially for the dry landscapes of Australia.

Little and large

Saddle up and see how different horses and ponies can be! The Shire is as tall as an adult man, but the sweet Shetland is shorter than a two-year-old child.

Height is measured from the withers (between the shoulders) to the hooves.

Shire horse

Massive and mighty, this **heavyweight horse** was once put to work pulling loads on farms.

Powerful and muscular body suited to hard work

Thick long hair, called feathers, covers the horse's huge hooves.

Horses and ponies are measured in **hands**. One hand is **4 in** (10.2 cm).

Strong neck muscles beneath thick skin and hair

Heavy horses
The biggest breeds have been used as workhorses since ancient times.

Light horses
With speed and stamina, these medium-sized horses are best for riding.

Ponies
Ponies are small horses that measure less than 14.2 hands (57 in/ 147 cm).

Shetland pony
Shetlands are truly **short and sweet**. This beautiful breed is the tiniest pony of all.

The small body is strong and sturdy.

How horses **work**

Horses are among the most beautiful creatures on Earth. Their powerhouse bodies move fast and freely. Throughout history, they have proven to be hardworking and helpful.

Coat
The coat comes in a wide variety of colors and patterns.

Tail
A thick tail of hair grows from the bony backside of the horse.

Hooves
Horses' hooves are hard but have to be protected with metal horseshoes to prevent damage.

Follow the leader

Once they've eaten all the grass, horses have to move on to new pastures. The leader decides when it is time for fresh grazing.

Snuggle buddies

A horsey friendship is sealed when horses stand close together to **nuzzle and clean** each other.

Boss moms

A mare (female horse) is in charge of each herd. Elephants are another animal whose groups are led by a female.

Cool
coat colors

Horses come in gleaming coats of many colors. They range from pure white to coal black. Brown horses are not forgotten, with lots of words to describe different chocolatey coats.

Bay
Bays are brown with black manes and tails.

Red roan
Horses with brown skin and white hair have a reddish tint called red roan.

Chestnut
Shades of rich red are called chestnut coats.

Black
Entirely black horses are uncommon.

Dun
A dun horse is sandy beige with a dark stripe down its back.

Gray
White horses are called grays!

Palomino
The palomino is a golden wonder, with its white mane and tail.

Brown
"Brown" horses are dark brown or nearly black. They are darker than bays.

Blue roan
Horses with black skin and white hair have a blue tint called blue roan.

15

Patterns and markings

Although some horses are one solid color, others have striking patterns. From the coat to the face, every horse is unique.

A dorsal stripe is a line of dark hair along the horse's backbone.

Face markings
Shapes and strips make it easy to tell horses apart. Learn and look out for these facial features.

White face
This all-white wonder is a face completely covered in white hair.

Blaze
What the blazes is this? A broad white strip right down the horse's muzzle!

Snip
Blink and you'll miss this one! The snip is a tiny little white patch between the nostrils.

Coat patterns

These patterned horses really know how to stand out at the stables...

Piebald

A patchy black-and-white coat

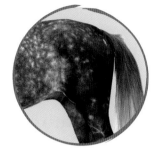

Dapple

A gray coat with patches of lighter hair

Appaloosa

A stunning coat of dark spots

Star

A star is born! White markings between the eyes may be loosely in the shape of a star.

Stripe

Narrower than a blaze, a stripe is a long, pale patch stretching from above the eyes to the nostrils.

Super senses

Horses are sensory superstars in the animal kingdom. They can see, hear, and smell much better than we can. Check out their sharp and sensitive senses.

Eye see!
The horse can see in almost all directions, but stay out of the "blind spot" to its rear so you don't startle it.

The long tail is used to whisk away flies.

Touchy-feely
A horse is sensitive to even the lightest touch, with muscles twitching as soon as a fly lands on its skin.

Listen up!
The big, perky ears can swivel around 180 degrees to follow the direction of sounds.

✔ Top tip

✔ **Top tip**

Don't make loud noises around horses. Noises can scare them because their hearing is highly sensitive.

Hold your nose!

If you ever see a horse that looks like it's laughing, look closer. When the head is raised and the lips are curled back to reveal the teeth, the horse is actually checking out a smell.

The horse's whiskers act as feelers around the nose to search the surroundings.

How horses **move**

A horse moves in four different ways, called gaits. The slowest gait is walking, which builds up to the fastest, the galloping gait.

Walk
Moving slowly and steadily is the most natural gait for a horse.

Gallop
The horse stretches its legs fully to go for the gallop. Hitting top speed takes a lot of energy.

The rider should stay relaxed and go with the rhythm.

20

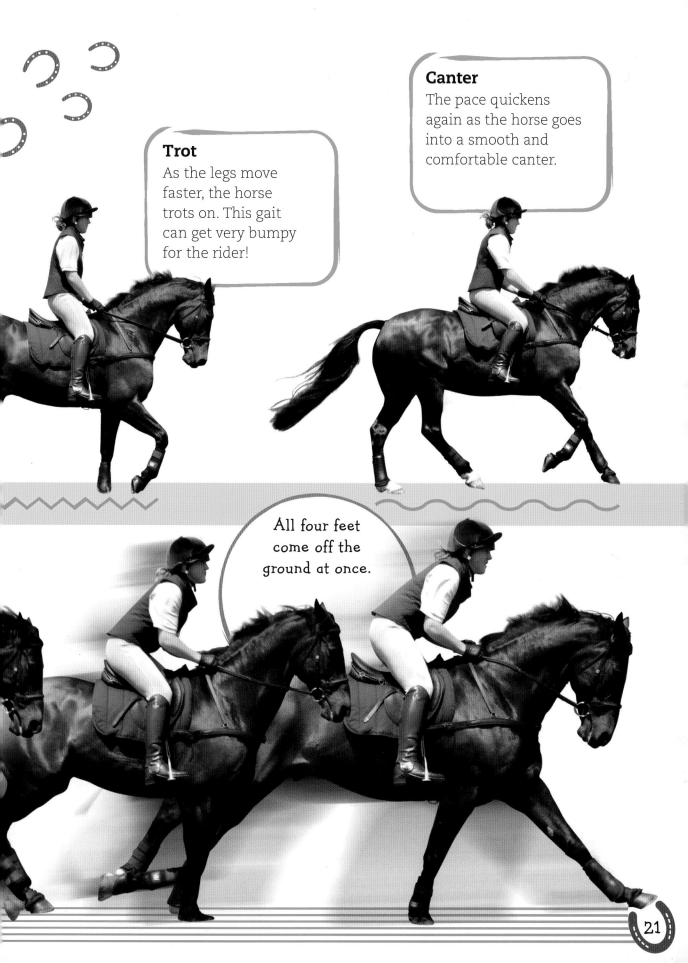

Trot
As the legs move faster, the horse trots on. This gait can get very bumpy for the rider!

Canter
The pace quickens again as the horse goes into a smooth and comfortable canter.

All four feet come off the ground at once.

Can a horse **talk?**

You won't get a great conversation straight from the horse's mouth! Horses use their bodies to express how they feel. Once you learn to read the signs, you'll know your horse so much better.

Ears pricked
From nose to tail, a horse reveals its mood without even realizing it. This horse is an eager beaver who wants to join in on the action.

One ear forward, one ear back
This horse is trying to keep an ear on two interesting things at once. If both ears are flattened, it means the horse is worried.

Head down low
This horse could be telling you it is happy to do as you ask. Or maybe it's in a relaxed mood, which borders on dozing off.

Sound decoder

Neigh
Horses make this loud sound when they are looking for or calling out to other horses or humans.

Snort
Something has startled this horse! Horses snort when they are not sure if something new is dangerous.

Nicker
Well, hello there! Horses may make this vibrating sound to greet their owners or other horses.

Pawing the ground
Come on, hurry up! This horse is bored with standing around waiting for you to be ready and wants to get moving.

Baring teeth
You have been warned! Leave this horse alone or you might get a bite.

Kicking out
Horses are not naturally aggressive animals, but this means "back off!" This horse is probably scared or spooked by something unexpected.

23

Perfect personalities

Horses are known for being clever, kind, and gentle creatures. They also each have their own special personalities. Let's meet the three main horse and pony personality types.

Hotbloods
These **fast-moving** horses from the hotter regions are emotional, loving, spirited, and curious.

Coldbloods
By contrast, **heavier horses** from the cold regions tend to be cool customers. They are calm, quiet, and patient.

Warmbloods
The energetic warmbloods blend the **athletic build** of the hotbloods with the **calm personality** of the coldbloods.

Remember to be patient

Don't lose patience with tricky horses. If you treat and train them well, they will reward you with their friendship. Horses remember kindness and are loyal to their owners.

Basic instincts

Don't forget that horses are naturally nervous and alert to any threat. When horses do not feel comfortable, they may take flight and run.

Enjoy the ride

Beginners and young children learn best on a calm, "cold-blooded" horse or pony.

Horsey hair care

It's not all **horseplay**, you know! After frolicking in the fields or cantering in competitions, horses need lots of **care**. Here is your guide to **good grooming**.

A dandy brush can be used to remove dirt and dust. Use very gently, and never on clipped coats.

Cleaning up

Horses need to be washed and brushed, just like we do. Owners must work hard to keep their horses clean and healthy.

A sponge soaked in warm water cleans the skin to leave the horse feeling fresh.

The mane grows down a horse's neck. This long hair is braided or brushed to prevent tangles.

Sweat scraper

Horses get hot, so this tool comes in handy to scrape away the sweat.

Currycomb

This metal comb loosens caked mud stuck to the body.

Dandy brush

All the dirt and hair on the surface are removed with this bristly brush.

Body brush
This brush is good for clipped coats and more sensitive areas.

Mane comb

Manes can get matted without the daily use of combs and brushes.

Hoof pick

This sharp tool is used to pick out any stones stuck in the hooves.

Hoof oil and brush
Brushing special oil onto the hooves protects them and adds shine.

New shoes
A horse's hooves are made from keratin, the same stuff as our hair and nails. Hooves can be cut without hurting the horse. Metal shoes stop hooves from being worn down too much on hard roads.

Horsey **homes**

Like all creatures, horses need a safe home to call their own. They like room to roam, and a place to shelter from the rain. Fresh water and food make the ideal home complete.

Paddock

Most horses spend part of the year outdoors in a fenced field called a paddock, where they can graze on grass.

Horse box

Special trailers called **horse boxes** are used to transport horses between stables and competitions.

A ramp makes it easy to walk in and out of the horse box.

Stables

Stables are solid, indoor **shelters**, but horses must still be taken out regularly for exercise.

Stabled horses like to look out over the top half of the stable door.

Horses can get lonely, so it is better if a few share the same paddock.

Equine eats

Horses are big beasts, with stomachs to match. Most of their time is spent grazing, and some breeds can munch their way through more than 26 lb (12 kg) of food in a single day.

Grass is greener

The most important part of a horse's daily diet is fresh grass, or dried grass called hay. A field for grazing is the best thing for horses.

Feeding facts

Dos and don'ts of horse feeding

Hard feed
If a horse is racing or jumping, it may need hard feed as well as grass. Hard feed is a mix of cereals and vitamins for an energy boost.

Treat time
Fruits and vegetables are welcomed by horses, although they should be saved for special occasions. Carrots and apples are the perfect treat.

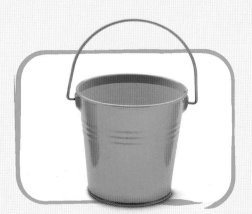

Water supply
A clean and fresh water supply is essential. Thirsty horses gulp down 12 gallons (45 liters) every day.

Poisonous plants
Take note of what is growing in your field—some plants and flowers are harmful to horses.

Weight check
If you can see your horse's ribs, it is probably underweight. If there are areas of fat along the neck, it needs less feed and more exercise.

Enjoy the **ride!**

Riding is a popular pastime, bringing fun and freedom to horse enthusiasts everywhere. Just make sure you have the right equipment to stay safe on your steed.

A hard helmet protects the rider's head in case of a fall.

The strong saddle cushions the rider's body and helps the horse carry her weight.

Equipped equine

Riding gear is designed to keep the rider safe, but it also considers the comfort of the horse.

Stirrups
Metal footrests called stirrups are attached to the saddle to support the feet.

Reins

Gently pulling on the reins lets the horse know whether to turn left, go right, or stop.

The reins attach to a piece of metal in the horse's mouth, called a bit.

Rodeo

Yee-haw! A rodeo is a cowboy contest in which competitors display their riding skills on a bucking bronco.

Sports **day**

Show jumpers have to jump fences in a set time and try to score the most points. Some courses focus on speed and accuracy, while others tackle tricky terrain.

Vertical jump

Most competitions include vertical jumps. The slightest touch can knock the poles off the frame.

Gymkhana

Younger riders can compete on ponies in events called gymkhanas. Children can showcase their riding and horse-handling skills over timed courses—and have fun, too!

Water jump

The horse and rider have to jump a long way to get over the water jump. If they touch the water, they will lose points.

Wall with bricks

The bricks in the wall are made of foam, not stone! Knocking even one brick out costs the rider points.

You and **your horse**

Take the reins! Horses are used to living in herds and like having a strong leader to follow. If you are lucky enough to own a horse, keep your pet healthy and happy with these tips.

Owner checklist

My pet horse

☐ Horses respond to a gentle approach—walk up to them from the side, quietly and casually. Hold out your hand and speak with kindness.

☐ Introduce anything new slowly. Let your horse sniff, touch, walk around, and explore new items of clothing or food until it feels comfortable.

☐ Even if your horse is not enthusiastic about some parts of training, keep doing it. Over time, your horse will get used to training, and this will become a normal part of your everyday routine.

☐ When your horse responds well to training, give it rewards. This can be a stroke, food, or just encouragement to show that you are proud of its efforts.

Health check

Spend a few minutes before every ride feeling the body and legs to see if your horse shows any signs of pain or illness. Signs of sickness include cold ears or a lack of energy. If you are worried, call the vet to be on the safe side.

Top training

Training builds trust and a strong bond between horse and owner. Practice leading and catching your horse in a field before moving on to more advanced training.

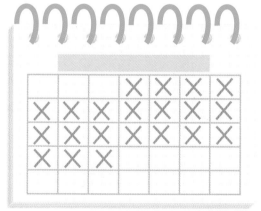

Creature of habit

Like all pets, horses need a set routine to follow. If you are always there for your pet, it will quickly come to love you and be very loyal. Whether with humans or other horses, always remember horses are sociable and love company.

Hardworking helpers

Horses never shy away from hard work. Their physical strength, willingness to learn, and ability to follow instructions have seen them take on tasks that people find challenging and exhausting.

Farmhands

For thousands of years, horses plowed the soil and carried loads on farms. Some farms in remote areas still rely on horses.

Horsey heroes

Some horses have proven themselves to be even tougher, braver, or faster than the rest of their species.

Comanche

A horse named Comanche was the only survivor from the US army when it fought the Lakota Sioux at the Battle of Little Big Horn in 1876.

Cowboys

In the US, cowboys ride on horseback to round up their cattle on huge ranches. They can be on their horses for up to 15 hours a day.

Police patrol

Police horses are trained to stay calm despite any noises and distractions around them. They often work at sporting events and public parades.

Sergeant Reckless

The warhorse Sergeant Reckless carried supplies to soldiers in the Korean War (1950–1953). She kept going despite being injured twice.

Red Rum

Record-breaking racehorse Red Rum won England's famous Grand National race three times—in 1973, 1974, and 1977.

Horses and **humans**

We have shared a close bond with our horsey friends throughout history. In the present day, horses are still ready to help us in times of need.

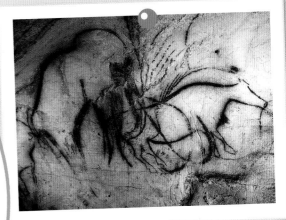

Stone Age cave art
Pictures of horses from more than **15,000 years ago** have been found in European caves.

1000 years BCE
Ancient kings showed off their wealth and power by riding to royal hunts in horse-drawn **chariots**.

Ancient Greece
The winged horse **Pegasus** appeared in ancient Greek mythology.

Medieval Europe
Horses carried heavily armored **knights** into war during the medieval period.

Heart and mind

Did you know that hanging out with horses can make you feel healthier and less stressed?

 Stroking a horse can make you feel calm. Visit your horse for lots of petting and together time.

 Riding a horse has been proven to make people feel happier. It's also great exercise.

 Horses love to try new games. Play with your horse to keep both of your brains exercised and alert.

Riding therapy
Learning to ride a pony can help children with physical and learning disabilities to manage their conditions. Riding builds confidence and brings a great sense of achievement.

Victorian era
In the 19th century, wealthy people traveled around in **horse-drawn carriages.** These were eventually replaced by cars.

 41

Light horses

Hold on tight! Light horses have long legs that are **perfect for running**. In the past, they pulled carriages and carts. Today, light horses perform in riding and racing competitions.

Tail sits high on the body.

Build is smaller than a heavy horse, but bigger than a pony.

Light horses are a variety of **sizes and colors.**

Flowing mane covering long neck

Strong, athletic legs for galloping

Thoroughbreds can run up to **40 mph (64 kph)**.

Thoroughbred
The world's fastest horse is the Thoroughbred, with its body built for speed, strength, and stamina.

Arabian

This beautiful breed once lived in the deserts of Asia and is one of the world's **oldest horses**. Famous figures from history rode Arabian horses for their graceful gait and super stamina.

The neck is long and arching.

The Arabian carries its tail high.

The head is quite small compared to the huge body.

Strong and powerful legs

Fact file

⚜ **Origin:** Arabian Peninsula

↗ **Height:** Up to 15 hands

⚖ **Weight:** 1,000 lb (450 kg)

❋ **Color:** Varies, but usually bay, chestnut, or gray

◉ **Characteristics:** Clever, brave, proud, tough, and energetic

◗ **Good for:** Riding, racing, and endurance

Akhal-Teke

A shining star of the horse world is the Akhal-Teke, known for the **sparkling sheen** on its coat. Lightning-fast, it makes a speedy racehorse.

Long ears sit in an alert position.

Special glossy hair gives the coat a metallic look.

Athletic body is built for speed.

White markings are often seen on the legs.

Fact file

🜨 **Origin:** Turkmenistan and Russia

↗ **Height:** Up to 16 hands

⚖ **Weight:** 1,000 lb (450 kg)

❀ **Color:** Usually black or bay

◐ **Characteristics:** Strong, sensitive, gentle, bold, and loyal

◑ **Good for:** Riding, racing, competition, eventing, and endurance

Thoroughbred

As one of the world's fastest animals, this record-breaking racehorse is sure to cross the finish line first. The Thoroughbred is a powerful breed and can run as fast as a car, at 40 mph (64 kph)!

Thoroughbreds have an elegant head and longer neck than most breeds.

Thoroughbred horses are called hot-blooded because they are quick and athletic.

Slim, lightweight body is packed with muscles.

This breed usually has **facial markings**.

Strong, long legs move quickly and easily.

Fact file

- 🌍 **Origin:** England
- ↗ **Height:** Up to 17 hands
- ⚖ **Weight:** 1,000 lb (450 kg)
- ✺ **Color:** Varies widely
- ⬭ **Characteristics:** Strong, sensitive, bold, enthusiastic, and energetic
- 🧭 **Good for:** Competitions, racing, and jumping

Welsh **cob**

Smaller than a horse but larger than a pony, compact cobs are typically **sure-footed** and **sturdy**. This hardy breed developed in the tough terrain of the Welsh countryside.

Strong neck muscles

Smaller head than most breeds

Powerful body enables high jumping.

Short, stocky legs move quickly.

Fact file

🧭 **Origin:** Wales

📐 **Height:** At least 13 hands

⚖ **Weight:** 1,000 lb (450 kg)

❋ **Color:** Variety of solid colors

◐ **Characteristics:** Clever, friendly, enthusiastic, loyal, and reliable

◕ **Good for:** Competition, trekking, and children's riding

Orlov trotter

Ridden by **royals** in centuries past, the Orlov trotter is still the pride of Russia today. This horse is a winning combination of elegant beauty, strength, and power.

Lightweight but power-packed body

Broad, powerful chest

Thick tail

Gray coat lightens as the horse ages.

Well-defined legs with visible joints

Fact file

🌐 **Origin:** Russia

↗ **Height:** Up to 17 hands

⚖ **Weight:** 1,000 lb (450 kg)

🎨 **Color:** Usually gray

🛡 **Characteristics:** Quiet, adaptable, reliable, clever, and gentle

🐎 **Good for:** Harness racing and riding

49

Trakehner

This handsome horse takes its name from the town in Prussia where it was first bred, 300 years ago. Now, this **agile athlete** is making a comeback in competitions, displaying its famously light, floating trot.

Muscular back

Long neck and elegant head

Lightweight body shape

Fact file

⊕ **Origin:** Prussia, now part of Poland

⊿ **Height:** Up to 17 hands

⬤ **Weight:** 1,200 lb (540 kg)

✺ **Color:** Variety of solid colors, but mainly black

◖ **Characteristics:** Bold, reliable, clever, adaptable, and willing

◖ **Good for:** Riding and competitions

Holsteiner

The sporty and stylish Holsteiner horse is a **natural winner** at equestrian competitions. It can leap over incredibly high fences and often competes in the Olympics and other sports events.

Powerful body

Strong and nimble feet

Muscular and athletic back legs

Fact file

- **Origin:** Germany
- **Height:** Up to 17 hands
- **Weight:** 1,025 lb (465 kg)
- **Color:** Varied, but mainly black and brown

- **Characteristics:** Brave, bold, willing, reliable, and sensitive
- **Good for:** Riding and competitions

Lipizzan

The dazzling dancers of the equestrian world are the Lipizzan horses. This rare breed is best known for its **dressage displays,** in which the horse performs precise movements to music.

The coat starts out dark before lightening to become the well-known white.

Fact file

- **Origin:** Spain
- **Height:** Up to 16 hands
- **Weight:** 1,150 lb (520 kg)
- **Color:** Almost always white
- **Characteristics:** Friendly, calm, clever, willing, and reliable
- **Good for:** Dressage and general riding

Muscular, agile legs suitable for controlled steps

Fast-moving feet look as though the horse is dancing.

Quarter horse

Saddle up, cowboys! The US's very first breed was the quarter horse. This **hardworking horse** was used for farming and still works on ranches. Although fairly small in size, it has lots of strength, speed, and stamina.

Short, muscular body

Strong, sturdy legs for sprinting

Fact file

🧭 **Origin:** USA

↗ **Height:** Up to 16 hands

⚖ **Weight:** 1,070 lb (485 kg)

❀ **Color:** Varies widely

🏵 **Characteristics:** Clever, calm, relaxed, adaptable, and gentle

🐎 **Good for:** Riding and sprinting

Andalusian

The Andalusian is a true picture of elegance. A close relation of the Lipizzan breed, this **strong and speedy** horse shares its beautiful cousin's looks and skills.

This breed is shown in ancient cave paintings in Spain.

Long, arched neck

Wavy, thick tail

Strong and powerful build

Fact file

- 🌍 **Origin:** Spain
- ↗ **Height:** Up to 16 hands
- 🏋 **Weight:** 1,200 lb (540 kg)
- ✳ **Color:** Usually gray

- ⭕ **Characteristics:** Clever, calm, gentle, energetic, and even-tempered
- 🐎 **Good for:** General riding, classical riding, dressage

Irish sports horse

Try to keep up with this **great galloper!** Used for foxhunting in the past, this horse is a super sprinter and always on the move.

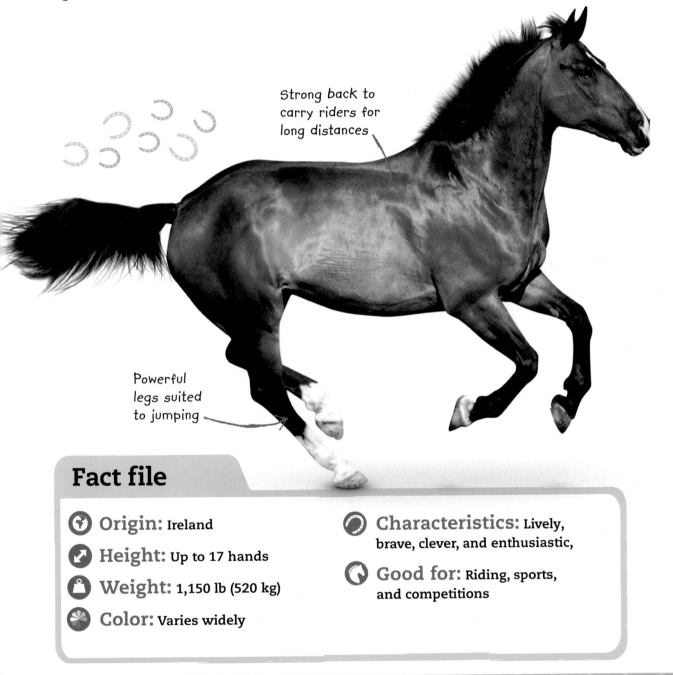

Strong back to carry riders for long distances

Powerful legs suited to jumping

Fact file

- 🌐 **Origin:** Ireland
- ↗ **Height:** Up to 17 hands
- ⚖ **Weight:** 1,150 lb (520 kg)
- ❂ **Color:** Varies widely
- ◎ **Characteristics:** Lively, brave, clever, and enthusiastic,
- ◖ **Good for:** Riding, sports, and competitions

Appaloosa

A leopard cannot change its spots, but this stunning breed certainly can! Baby Appaloosas are often born plain and their spots develop as they grow. The vibrant coat patterns have names such as leopard, snowflake, and marble.

Unique coat can be totally covered in spots.

Appaloosas have starred in many cowboy movies and television shows.

Black and pink
mottled skin is
a feature of
the face.

Fact file

🌐 **Origin:** USA

↗ **Height:** Up to 15 hands

⚖ **Weight:** Up to 1,250 lb
(565 kg)

❁ **Color:** Variety of colors
and patterns

🌀 **Characteristics:** Clever,
calm, reliable, adaptable,
and willing

🐎 **Good for:** Riding and racing

Striped
hooves

Heavy horses

Stand back! Heavy load coming through... Think **big** when it comes to the heavy horses. These hard workers have carried large loads throughout history.

Massive hooves spread the horse's weight.

Most heavy horses are **gentle giants**.

Powerful back and neck muscles for pulling and carrying

Long, thick hair creates a feathered look over feet.

Shire horses can pull up to **5½ tons (5 metric tons)**.

Shire horse
The world's biggest breed is Britain's super-sized Shire.

Friesian

This black beauty from the Netherlands is a hardworking, **heavyweight horse**. The strong Friesian carried armored knights into battle in medieval times.

Head held high on a long, arched neck

Long, luxurious mane

Strong and muscular body

Fact file

- **Origin:** Netherlands
- **Height:** Up to 17 hands
- **Weight:** 1,450 lb (655 kg)
- **Color:** Black

- **Characteristics:** Willing, gentle, affectionate, loyal, and dependable
- **Good for:** Riding, pulling carriages, and dressage

Schleswig

The strong and sturdy Schleswig is happy to do the hard work. In the past, its list of jobs included pulling buses and trolleys, working the land, and dragging wood.

Compact body is powerful and muscular.

Strong legs suited to easy, agile movement

Fact file

- **Origin:** Germany
- **Height:** Up to 16 hands
- **Weight:** 1,400 lb (635 kg)
- **Color:** Mainly chestnut

- **Characteristics:** Eager, calm, sweet-natured, willing, and reliable
- **Good for:** Riding and farmwork

Belgian draft

This big Belgian is packed with **superhero strength**. The breed was first used for heavy farmwork and is still the most popular draft horse (horse that pulls carts and loads) in the US.

Large, powerful body can pull heavy loads easily.

Strong, lean legs

Huge hooves

Fact file

⦿ **Origin:** Belgium

⦿ **Height:** Up to 17 hands

⦿ **Weight:** 2,000 lb (900 kg)

⦿ **Color:** Mainly chestnut or bay

⦿ **Characteristics:** Gentle, willing, reliable, sweet-natured, and hardworking

⦿ **Good for:** Farmwork and draft (pulling) competitions

Breton

The Breton is a **gentle giant** among the big breeds. It is named after the Brittany region of France, where it was first developed. It worked in the vineyards where wine is made.

Stocky body with heavyweight bones

Short legs are muscular and feathered.

Fact file

- 🌐 **Origin:** France
- 📏 **Height:** Up to 16 hands
- ⚖️ **Weight:** 1,750 lb (800 kg)
- 🎨 **Color:** Mainly chestnut or red roan
- 🏇 **Characteristics:** Gentle, friendly, energetic, reliable, and calm
- 🐎 **Good for:** Farmwork and riding

Rhineland
heavy draft

Once Germany's most popular type of horse, the Rhineland heavy draft is now more rare but still well loved. This **huge and hairy** breed is great at pulling carriages.

The Rhinelander is a slimmer breed that was developed from the Rhineland heavy draft.

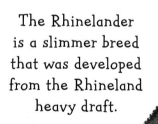

Fact file

- 🌍 **Origin:** Germany
- ↗ **Height:** Up to 17 hands
- ⚖ **Weight:** 2,200 lb (1,000 kg)
- ❋ **Color:** Mainly chestnut
- ◠ **Characteristics:** Quiet, willing, energetic, calm, and sweet-natured
- ◷ **Good for:** Farmwork

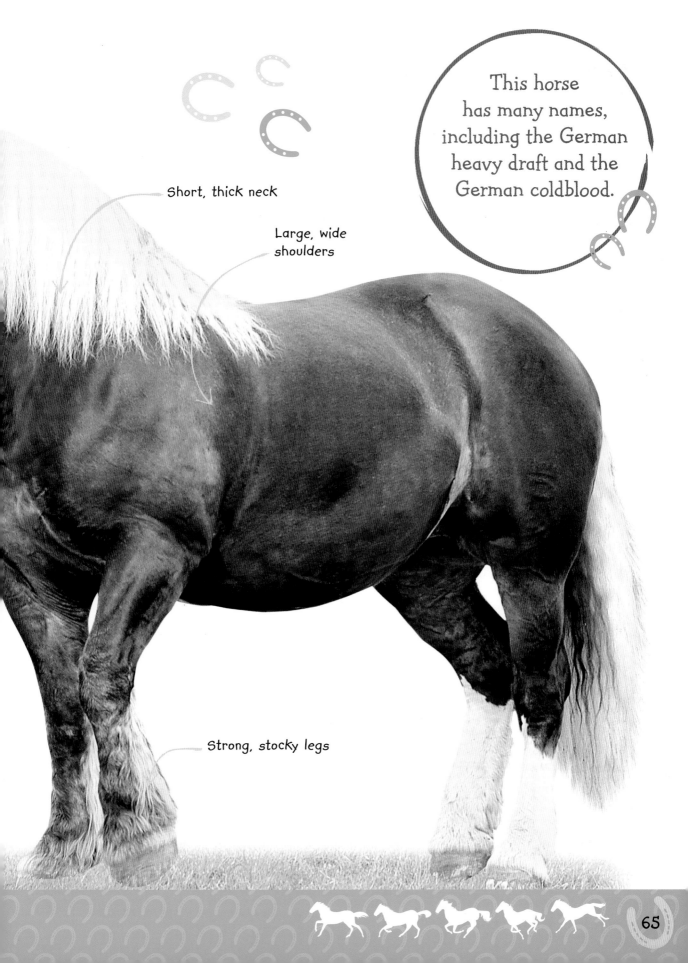

Short, thick neck

Large, wide shoulders

This horse has many names, including the German heavy draft and the German coldblood.

Strong, stocky legs

Percheron

France has more breeds of heavy horse than any other country, with the perfect Percheron the best known of them all. This horse moves **elegantly** and is friendly and helpful.

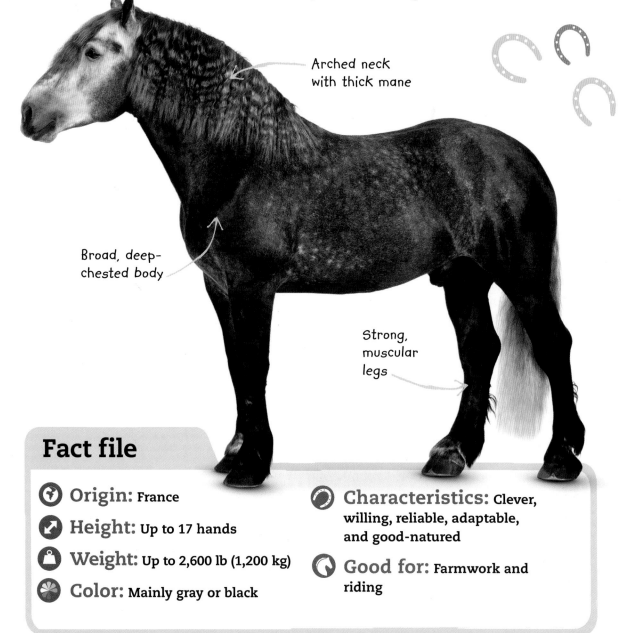

Arched neck with thick mane

Broad, deep-chested body

Strong, muscular legs

Fact file

🌐 **Origin:** France

↗ **Height:** Up to 17 hands

⚖ **Weight:** Up to 2,600 lb (1,200 kg)

❀ **Color:** Mainly gray or black

🐎 **Characteristics:** Clever, willing, reliable, adaptable, and good-natured

🌀 **Good for:** Farmwork and riding

Clydesdale

Although huge in size, the Clydesdale is ultimately a **big softie!** This horse has strength, stamina, and sweetness in equal measure.

One Clydesdale horse can pull the weight of two cars!

White markings on the face

Thick legs, huge hooves, and heavy white feathering on the legs

Fact file

- **Origin:** Scotland
- **Height:** Up to 16 hands
- **Weight:** Up to 2,200 lb (1,000 kg)
- **Color:** Mostly bay
- **Characteristics:** Active, energetic, kind, loyal, and gentle
- **Good for:** Farmwork and pulling loads

Norwegian fjord

A striped mane makes this horse **stand out from the crowd**. The Norwegian fjord is super friendly and willing to do any job required in the rugged terrain of its native country.

Dorsal stripe stands upright down the middle of the mane.

Tail is darker than the main body color.

Horizontal stripes, like a zebra, on the legs

Fact file

- 🌍 **Origin:** Norway
- 🐎 **Height:** Up to 14 hands
- ⚖ **Weight:** 1,200 lb (540 kg)
- 🎨 **Color:** Mainly dun, but can be red, gray, white, or yellow
- 🏵 **Characteristics:** Friendly, clever, athletic, patient, lively, and willing
- 🏇 **Good for:** Farmwork, riding, competitions, and dressage

Australian stock

Nicknamed "the breed for every need," this **tough cookie** is up for taking part in a variety of work, sports, and competitions.

Long, arched neck

Broad,
powerful
shoulders

Sturdy,
strong body

Fact file

- **Origin:** Australia
- **Height:** Up to 16 hands
- **Weight:** 1,200 lb (540 kg)
- **Color:** Varies, but mostly bay

- **Characteristics:** Clever, athletic, even-tempered, lively, and willing
- **Good for:** Herding cattle, competitions, dressage, and sports

Shire horse

Make way for the big one! The Shire is the world's **biggest and heaviest** horse. In medieval times, Shires carried heavily armored knights as they jousted with lances.

Wide, white strip called a blaze down the muzzle

Powerful body packed with muscles

Fact file

- **Origin:** England
- **Height:** Up to 18 hands
- **Weight:** Up to 2,500 lb (1,130 kg)
- **Color:** Mainly black or bay
- **Characteristics:** Sweet-natured, gentle, hardworking, calm, and reliable
- **Good for:** Farmwork, pulling carriages, and riding

Long, muscly legs are great for pulling heavy loads.

Suffolk punch

The chunky Suffolk punch is great at working in muddy ground because it doesn't have feathery feet. The breed comes from one stallion born in 1768 in Suffolk, England.

Coat is always chestnut color, but can be light or dark.

Short, muscular legs can pull huge weights

Feet are unusual for a heavy horse because they are not feathered.

Fact file

⊕ **Origin:** England

↗ **Height:** Up to 16 hands

⬚ **Weight:** 2,200 lb (1,000 kg)

✳ **Color:** Chestnut

◗ **Characteristics:** Energetic, dependable, hardworking, focused, and gentle

◗ **Good for:** Farmwork, pulling carriages, and forestry

Donkey

The domesticated ass, better known as the donkey, first carried loads across the **Sahara Desert**. This close relation of horses and zebras has been working for humans for more than 5,000 years.

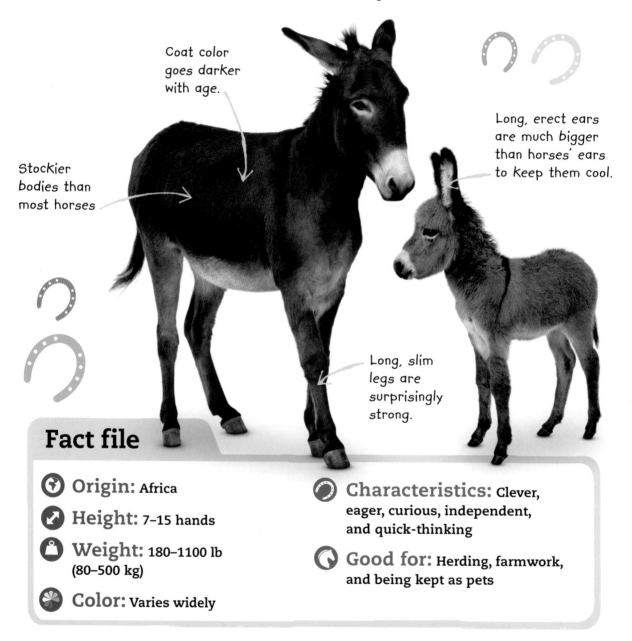

Coat color goes darker with age.

Long, erect ears are much *bigger* than horses' ears to keep them cool.

Stockier bodies than most horses

Long, slim legs are surprisingly strong.

Fact file

- 🌍 **Origin:** Africa
- ↗ **Height:** 7–15 hands
- ⚖ **Weight:** 180–1100 lb (80–500 kg)
- ⚫ **Color:** Varies widely

- 🛡 **Characteristics:** Clever, eager, curious, independent, and quick-thinking
- 🌀 **Good for:** Herding, farmwork, and being kept as pets

Mule

A mix of a **male donkey** and a **female horse** makes a mule. The Sumerian people of ancient Mesopotamia first bred mules about 4,000 years ago. They are perfect for carrying supplies.

Longer ears typical of a donkey

Thick skin can withstand extreme temperatures.

Heavier head than most donkeys

Slim legs and small hooves like a donkey's

Fact file

🌍 **Origin:** Mesopotamia (modern-day Iraq and Turkey)

↗ **Height:** Up to 15 hands

⚖ **Weight:** Up to 1,000 lb (450 kg)

❁ **Color:** Varies widely

🛡 **Characteristics:** Patient, sociable, clever, and careful

🐴 **Good at:** Hauling loads

Ponies

Pretty little ponies and dainty miniature horses are the perfect size for **children** to ride. Ponies are less than 14.2 hands high.

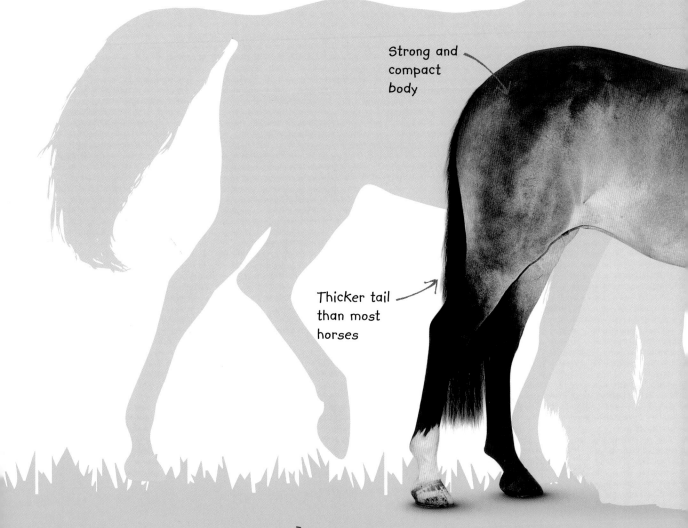

Strong and compact body

Thicker tail than most horses

There are more than **200 breeds** of pony.

Small, alert ears

Ponies have roamed England's **New Forest** since the **11th century**.

Short, slim legs can move fast.

New Forest Pony
Although short in stature and sweet in nature, these ponies are surprisingly strong and sturdy.

Pony of the **Americas**

It's easy to spot this pretty pony. The **spotted-patterned** coat makes it stand out. First bred in the 1950s, this child-friendly pony is just the right height for you to ride!

The coat has dark spots like a leopard's, on a light background.

The short, slender legs are surprisingly strong and solid.

Hooves are unusual because they have colored stripes.

Fact file

Origin: USA

Height: 11.2 to 14 hands

Weight: 560 lb (255 kg)

Color: Appaloosa spot pattern

Characteristics: Friendly, quiet, strong, athletic, and reliable

Good for: Sports, racing, jumping, and riding for children

German riding pony

Giddyup for a race on the German riding pony! This **smooth runner** has all the speed and style of a horse, making it a natural champion in competitions.

The ears and head are small, like a typical pony's.

Long legs give this pony a wide and powerful stride.

Fact file

🎯 **Origin:** Germany

📏 **Size:** 13.2 to 14.2 hands

⚖️ **Weight:** Up to 880 lb (400 kg)

🌈 **Color:** White, black, brown, gray, and chestnut

🔵 **Characteristics:** Obedient, mild-tempered, willing, and clever

🔵 **Good at:** Dressage, show jumping, eventing, and pulling carriages

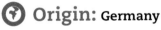

Welsh pony

This picture-perfect pony is among the most popular rides for children and often appears at horse shows. It is descended from the Arab horse and has the same elegant trot.

Larger eyes than most breeds

Slim, muscular legs move free and fast.

White markings are a common feature of Welsh ponies.

Fact file

🌍 **Origin:** Wales

↗ **Height:** Up to 14 hands

🏋 **Weight:** 500 lb (225 kg)

❋ **Color:** Variety

⭕ **Characteristics:** Energetic, friendly, eager, adaptable, and reliable

🔄 **Good for:** Riding, carrying light loads, and competitions

Highland pony

The Highland breed is no one-trick pony. As the largest British pony, it has the strength to carry large loads, pull wagons, and trek over long distances.

Strong, well-balanced body

Thick tail

Powerful legs and sure-footed hooves

Fact file

- **Origin:** Scotland
- **Height:** Up to 14 hands
- **Weight:** Up to 1,200 lb (550 kg)
- **Color:** Mainly gray or dun

- **Characteristics:** Calm, friendly, gentle, reliable, and active
- **Good for:** Farmwork, heavy lifting, and riding

Shetland pony

This petite pony is living proof that good things come in small packages. Although it is the **smallest** of the ancient pony breeds, the Shetland is surprisingly strong and tough.

Full mane

Fact file

- 🌐 **Origin:** Scotland
- 🐎 **Height:** Up to 11 hands
- ⚖️ **Weight:** Up to 440 lb (200 kg)
- 🎨 **Color:** Varies widely
- ⭕ **Characteristics:** Independent, strong-willed, reliable, tough, and friendly
- 🌍 **Good for:** Pulling carts, children's riding, and competitions

Double winter coat keeps the pony dry and warm.

Short legs

The Shetland pony can pull twice its own body weight.

Small but **superstrong**

Long, thick tail

Small, strong hooves

Fell pony

The Fell is a firm favorite among the pony breeds. With a long history of **carrying, pulling,** and **riding** in the mountains of northern England, this tough guy always keeps up the good work.

Smaller head compared to overall body size

Muscular body

Short legs

Tough, strong feet

Fact file

- 🌍 **Origin:** Britain
- ↗ **Height:** Up to 14 hands
- ⚖ **Weight:** 1,000 lb (450 kg)
- ✹ **Color:** Black, bay, or brown

- ⬭ **Characteristics:** Willing, intelligent, tough, curious, and adaptable
- 🐴 **Good for:** Riding and pulling carts

Newfoundland pony

This power-packed pony's ancestors arrived in Newfoundland, Canada, with **settlers** from Britain. Its list of jobs included hauling in fishing nets, plowing the soil, and transporting families.

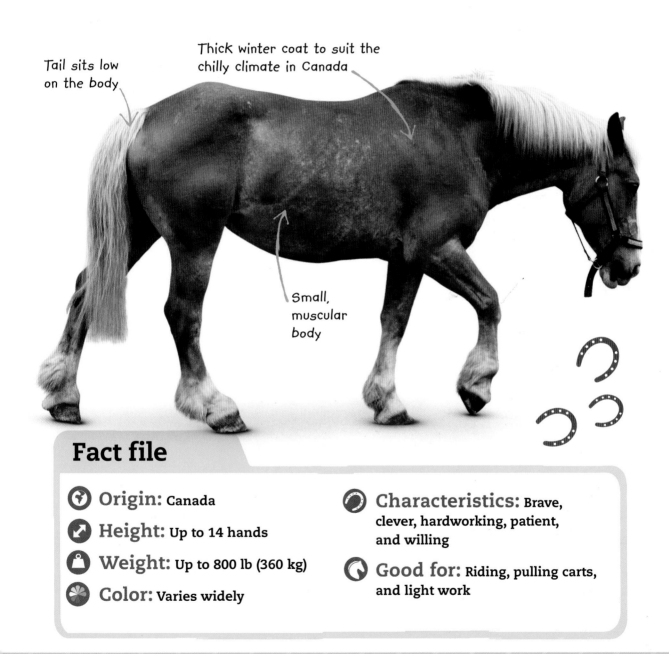

Tail sits low on the body

Thick winter coat to suit the chilly climate in Canada

Small, muscular body

Fact file

- 🧭 **Origin:** Canada
- 📐 **Height:** Up to 14 hands
- ⚖️ **Weight:** Up to 800 lb (360 kg)
- ❋ **Color:** Varies widely
- 🥎 **Characteristics:** Brave, clever, hardworking, patient, and willing
- 🌐 **Good for:** Riding, pulling carts, and light work

Icelandic horse

This unique breed is best known for having **five gaits**. While most horses walk, trot, canter, and maybe even gallop, the Icelandic superstar can also tölt, which is a fast walk.

Thick, messy mane

Double coat is the ideal winter warmer.

Fact file

- 🧭 **Origin:** Iceland
- ↗ **Height:** Up to 14 hands
- ⚖ **Weight:** 850 lb (380 kg)
- ❋ **Color:** Varies widely
- 🎨 **Characteristics:** Tough, clever, spirited, friendly, and independent
- 🐾 **Good for:** Herding sheep, competitions, and riding

Short, strong legs

Sandalwood pony

Welcome to paradise! The Sandalwood pony hails from the beautiful **Indonesian islands** of Sumba and Sumbawa. It is named after the sandalwood trees that grow there.

Strong, sturdy body

Slim, powerful legs

Fact file

🌐 **Origin:** Indonesia

📏 **Height:** Up to 13 hands

⚖️ **Weight:** 650 lb (300 kg)

🎨 **Color:** Variety

🧿 **Characteristics:** Friendly, willing, hardworking, easygoing, and energetic

🧭 **Good for:** Racing, riding, and farmwork

Haflinger

Meet the golden wonder of the Austrian mountains. The tiny Haflinger horse can stay **very calm** while crossing steep slopes and tricky terrain.

Eye-catching golden mane and tail

Gold sheen to the coat

Small but solid body

Fact file

- **Origin:** Austria
- **Height:** Up to 13 hands
- **Weight:** 1,100 lb (500 kg)
- **Color:** Chestnut or palamino

- **Characteristics:** Willing, sweet-natured, reliable, friendly, and curious
- **Good for:** Riding and driving

Falabella

The world's **smallest breed** of horse is the fabulous Falabella, which at 3 ft (1 m) tall is even tinier than the smallest pony, the Shetland.

Thick mane

Sleek, spotted coat is one of many colors and patterns.

Thick tail

Same weight as a large dog

Fact file

- **Origin:** Argentina
- **Height:** Up to 7.5 hands
- **Weight:** 100 lb (45 kg)
- **Color:** Varies widely
- **Characteristics:** Clever, adaptable, gentle, even-tempered, and loyal
- **Good for:** Children's riding

Hokkaido pony

Jump on this Japanese pony for an **off-road adventure!** The mountainous areas of Hokkaido Island cannot be reached by truck, but this pony provides the perfect transportation.

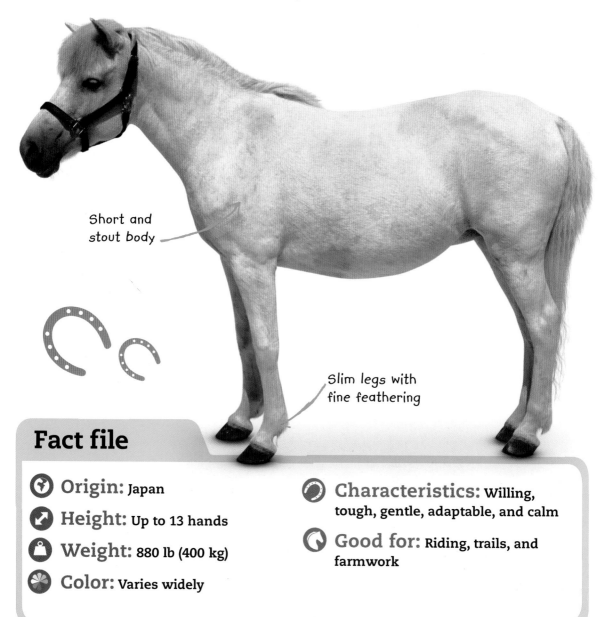

Short and stout body

Slim legs with fine feathering

Fact file

- **Origin:** Japan
- **Height:** Up to 13 hands
- **Weight:** 880 lb (400 kg)
- **Color:** Varies widely

- **Characteristics:** Willing, tough, gentle, adaptable, and calm
- **Good for:** Riding, trails, and farmwork

Australian pony

Say "G'day!" to this "bewt" little pony. Perfectly designed for **riding**, this gorgeous pony makes riding smooth sailing.

Small, muscular body

Short, strong legs

Fact file

🌐 **Origin:** Australia

📐 **Height:** Up to 14 hands

⚖ **Weight:** 600 lb (270 kg)

✳ **Color:** Varies widely

🛡 **Characteristics:** Alert, clever, good-natured, relaxed, and sensible

🌀 **Good at:** Riding and competitions

Quiz—what do you know about horses?

With hundreds of breeds of horses around the world, there's so much horsey knowledge to remember. Take this quiz to find out whether you know heaps about horses!

1. Which of these is the smallest horse in the world?

- ☐ **a)** Friesian
- ☐ **b)** Falabella
- ☐ **c)** Arabian

2. How long does it take for a horse to grow to its full size?

- ☐ **a)** Four years
- ☐ **b)** Ten years
- ☐ **c)** Twenty years

3. What do you call a female foal?

- ☐ **a)** A colt
- ☐ **b)** A mare
- ☐ **c)** A filly

4. Which of these is the fastest way a horse can move?

- ☐ **a)** Trot
- ☐ **b)** Gallop
- ☐ **c)** Canter

5. What are the perfect treats for a horse?

- ☐ **a)** Carrots and apples
- ☐ **b)** Chips and dip
- ☐ **c)** Cake and chocolate

6. Which of these is the fastest breed of horse?

- ☐ **a)** Shetland
- ☐ **b)** Belgian draft
- ☐ **c)** Thoroughbred

7. How are horses and ponies measured?

- ☐ **a)** in hands
- ☐ **b)** in feet
- ☐ **c)** in arms

Glossary

Affectionate Warm and loving.

Aggressive Angry and violent.

Ancient Very old.

Bit Piece of metal placed in a horse's mouth so a rider can guide it.

Breed Type of horse with specific characteristics.

Coldblooded Heavy horses from cold parts of the world.

Colt Young male horse.

Cowboy Man on horseback who herds and cares for cattle.

Domestic Animal that is taken care of by people.

Dressage Training a horse for riding competitions involving control and balance.

Equestrian Related to horseback riding.

Equine A horse or something that is horselike.

Feathering Long hair on the lower legs of some horses.

Filly Young female horse.

Foal Very young horse.

Grazing Nibbling at grass for food.

Grooming Caring for hair so it stays neat and clean.

Gymkhana Horse-riding competition for children.

Hand Measurement used for the height of a horse.

Harness racing Race where a horse or pony pulls a cart.

Herd Group of animals living together.

Hoof Horny foot of some mammals.

Horse box Vehicle used to transport a horse.

Hotblood Fast horses from hot parts of the world.

Mammal Hairy, warm-blooded creature, including horses and humans.

Mare Adult female horse.

Muzzle Nose and mouth of a horse.

Native Born or coming from a specific place.

Paddock Small field where horses live.

Plowing Turning over soil ready for farming.

Pony Small breed of equine under 14.2 hands.

Predator Animal that hunts other animals to eat.

Ranch Big farm used to keep or breed cattle.

Reins Leather straps used to guide a horse.

Rodeo Competition in which cowboys display their riding skills on horseback.

Saddle Seat for a rider to sit on a horse.

Stable Building to house a horse or several horses.

Stallion Adult male horse.

Stirrups Foot supports attached to a saddle by straps.

Trekking Riding across the countryside for several hours, usually on a pony.

Warmblood A horse of average weight combining characteristics of both the hotbloods and coldbloods.

Wild An animal living free without any help from people.

Index

Acknowledgments

DK would like to thank:
Sumedha Chopra for picture research; Eleanor Bates for additional design; Helen Peters for the index; Jolyon Goddard for proofreading; Sally Beets for additional editorial.

The publisher would like to thank the following for their kind permission to reproduce their photographs:

Key: a=above; b=below/bottom; c=center; f=far; l=left, r=right, t=top.

1 123RF.com: byrdyak. 3 123RF.com: Martha Snider (bl). **Alamy Stock Photo:** Moritz Wolf / imageBROKER (br). 4 **Dorling Kindersley:** Bob Langrish / Pegasus of Kilverstone Wildlife Park / Falabella pony (cb). 4-5 **Dreamstime.com:** Dreamzdesigner (c). 5 123RF.com: Carlos Caetano / ccaetano (bl). **Dorling Kindersley:** Bob Langrish / Bay, Mrs Scott, Hendon Caspian Stud (tr); Jerry Young (c). 5 123RF.com: Carlos Caetano / ccaetano (bl). **Dorling Kindersley:** Bob Langrish / Bay, Mrs Scott, Hendon Caspian Stud (tr); Jerry Young (c). **Dreamstime.com:** Hedrus (clb). 6 **Dorling Kindersley:** Bob Langrish / Jim Lockwood, Courage Shire Horse Centre, Berkshire. 7 **Dorling Kindersley:** Gary Ombler (br). 8-9 **Dreamstime.com:** Viacheslav Nemyrivskyi (c). 9 **Dreamstime.com:** Anjajuli (br); Jose Manuel Gelpi Diaz (tr); Anastasia Shapochkina (cr). 10 **Alamy Stock Photo:** Tierfotoagentur / R. Richter (tr, c, bl). 10-11 123RF.com: byrdyak (bc). 11 **Alamy Stock Photo:** Tierfotoagentur / R. Richter (tl, c); Tierfotoagentur / S. Starick (br). 12 123RF.com: Kseniya Abramova (cl). 12-13 iStockphoto.com: SimplyCreativePhotography (b). 13 123RF.com: Anastasija Popova (tr). 14 123RF.com: Rene van den Berg (br). **Dorling Kindersley:** Bob Langrish (c). **Dreamstime.com:** Viktoria Makarova / Bjakko (bl). 15 123RF.com: Svetlana Churkina (tr); Eric Isselee (cl); Viacheslav Nemyrivskyi (br). **Dreamstime.com:** Tamara Bauer (cr); Dawn Young (bl). 16 123RF.com: Robert Francis (cra). **Dorling Kindersley:** Bob Langrish / Spooks, Peter Munt, Ascot Driving Stables, Berks / Gelderlander Horse (cb); Bob Langrish / Hyppolyte, Haras National De Pau, Gelos 64110, Jurancon, France (crb). **Dreamstime.com:** Terry Alexander / Terdonal (clb). 17 123RF.com: Nigel Baker (cla). **Alamy Stock Photo:** Tierfotoagentur / C. Demmelbauer-Ebner (clb). 18 123RF.com: globalphoto (tr). **Depositphotos Inc:** okiepony (clb). 18-19 123RF.com: Martha Snider (bc). 19 **Dreamstime.com:** Pimmimemom (tl); Brad Sauter (cr). 22 123RF.com: Viktoria Makarova (cl). **Dreamstime.com:** Jacqueline Nix (bl); Pavlos Rekas / Preckas (crb). 23 123RF.com: Kseniya Abramova (crb); MembrÃ © Joffrey (tl). **Alamy Stock Photo:** Juniors Bildarchiv GmbH / R315 (bl); Carol Walker / naturepl.com (cl). 24 **Alamy Stock Photo:** MediaWorldImages (clb). **Dreamstime.com:** Kseniya Abramova / Tristana (cra). 25 **Alamy Stock Photo:** Juniors Bildarchiv GmbH / F368; Foto Grebler (clb). 27 **Dorling Kindersley:** Jerry Young (cb, ca). 28 123RF.com: Evgeniya Gappova (br); Zuzana Tillerova (cr); Dmytro Tolmachov (cb). 29 123RF.com: Ina van Hateren (cb); Zuzana Tillerova (tc, cb/Two white horses

); Golubenko Svetlana (tc/Horse); Mary R. Vogt (tr). 30 123RF.com: pitrs. 31 **Dreamstime.com:** Tracy Decourcy / Rimglow (cra); Chee Siong Teh / Tehcheesiong (cl); Olga Lipatova (br). 33 123RF.com: Margo Harrison (cb). 34 123RF.com: mreco99 (cl). 35 **Alamy Stock Photo:** Steven Roe (tl). 36 **Dreamstime.com:** Stocksolutions (r). 37 **Dreamstime.com:** Anna Cvetkova (tl). 38 **Alamy Stock Photo:** Andrzej Gorzkowski Photography (cl); The History Collection (bc). 38-39 **Dreamstime.com:** Customposterdesigns (c). 39 **Alamy Stock Photo:** Trinity Mirror / Mirrorpix (bc); PJF Military Collection (bl). **Dreamstime.com:** Nigel Spiers (r). 40 **Depositphotos Inc:** Kacpura (cl). **Dorling Kindersley:** The Trustees of the British Museum (bl); Philippe Giraud (tr); Royal Armouries, Leeds (br). 41 **Alamy Stock Photo:** PE Forsberg (bl); Nik Taylor (cl). 42-43 123RF.com: Golubenko Svetlana. 44 **Dreamstime.com:** John Furlotte. 45 **Dreamstime.com:** Maria Itina. 46-47 **Dorling Kindersley:** Bob Langrish / Lyphento, Conkwell Grange Stud, Avon. 46 **Dreamstime.com:** Kseniya Abramova / Tristana (bl). 47 **Dreamstime.com:** Accept001 (tr). 49 iStockphoto.com: olgaIT. 50 **Dreamstime.com:** Kseniya Abramova / Tristana. 51 iStockphoto.com: purple_queue. 52 iStockphoto.com: Somogyvari. 54 **Dreamstime.com:** Kseniya Abramova / Tristana. 55 **Alamy Stock Photo:** Juniors Bildarchiv GmbH / F368. 56 **Alamy Stock Photo:** Mark J. Barrett (bc). 56-57 123RF.com: Yulia Remezova. 57 **Dreamstime.com:** Adam Goss (tr). 58-59 123RF.com: Eric Isselee. 62 **Dreamstime.com:** Gerald Marella. 63 Kit Houghton / **Houghton's Horses.** 65 **Alamy Stock Photo:** Only Horses Tbk. 66 123RF.com: Eric Isselee. 67 iStockphoto.com: georgeclerk. 68 **Dorling Kindersley:** Bob Langrish / Ausdan Svejk, John Goddard Fenwick and Lyn Morgan, Ausden Stud, Dyfed. 70 **Dorling Kindersley:** Jerry Young. 71 **Dreamstime.com:** Nigel Baker. 72 **Dreamstime.com:** Eric Isselee. 73 **Dorling Kindersley:** Bob Langrish / Mammoth Mule, #Kentucky Horse Park. 77 **Alamy Stock Photo:** Panther Media GmbH. 78 123RF.com: Veronika Petrova. 79 **Dorling Kindersley:** Bob Langrish / Fruich of Dykes, Countess of Swinton, Dykes Hill House, Masham. 80-81 **Alamy Stock Photo:** ELF Photography. 83 **Alamy Stock Photo:** Stuart Forster (c). 84 **Alamy Stock Photo:** Moritz Wolf / imageBROKER. 86 **Dreamstime.com:** Lenkadan. 87 **Dorling Kindersley:** Bob Langrish / Pegasus of Kilverstone Wildlife Park / Falabella pony. 90 123RF.com: Nigel Baker (bl). **Alamy Stock Photo:** Tierfotoagentur / S. Starick (clb). **Dorling Kindersley:** Bob Langrish / Pegasus of Kilverstone Wildlife Park / Falabella pony (cl). 91 123RF.com: Petar Dojkic (cla); Anastasija Popova / virgonira (tl). 92 **Alamy Stock Photo:** ELF Photography (bl). 93 iStockphoto.com: olgaIT (bc). 94 **Dreamstime.com:** Viacheslav Nemyrivskyi (bc). 95 **Dreamstime.com:** Kseniya Abramova / Tristana (br); Maria Itina (bl). 96 **Dreamstime.com:** Eric Isselee (bc)

Cover images: Front: 123RF.com: mdorottya bl; Ardea: Jean-Michel Labat crb; Fotolia: Paul Cotney br, Eric Isselee cra; Back: Fotolia: Eric Isselee tc, Viorel Sima tr; iStockphoto.com: nycshooter tl; Warren Photographic Limited: br

All other images © Dorling Kindersley.
For further information see: www.dkimages.com